Inside [illegible] from the Chicago Police Force & Others

Written by:

Tony Cuttone

For More Information Contact:

Whitehall Publishing
P.O. Box 548
Yellville, AR 72687
http://www.whitehallpublishing.com
info@whitehallpublishing.com

Tony Cuttone
PO Box 816
Clinton, AR 72031
http://www.tonycuttone.com
info@tonycuttone.com

Cover Design:
Ascender Graphix
http://www.ascendergraphix.com

Printed in the U.S.A.
Retail Price: $12.95

Table Of Contents

Section One - Working Midnights

Section Two - Working Days

Section Three

Foreword

I decided to become a Policeman for the financial security it would provide for my family. So I joined the Chicago Police Department. In their training academy and in learning all the many traffic and criminal laws to be enforced, it was almost overwhelming.

"I have always believed that if you can't laugh, you have no life at all"
Tony Cuttone

Laughter is medicine. Many times you must find something to laugh at or smile at or you will end up crying. I think that is why I ended up with a warped sense of humor, as you will see while you read the stories in this book.

While working for the Chicago P.D. and the Cook County Sheriff's Police, I worked with some of the greatest, most professional Police Officers who were good at their jobs and able to keep their sense of humor through it all, in spite of the many terrible things they encountered on a daily basis. Working with the large population of Chicago and Cook County, the number of dangerous and humorous situations I encountered is beyond estimation.

Try to understand the different types of police calls you receive from a humorous 'assist citizen' to a deadly, tragic 'homicide' and how you must find a way to laugh or else you will cry.

When I finished work every day, I went home to my wife. I never told her about the serious cases, only the funny things that happened. I never wanted her to worry that I might not be coming home.

When I completed eleven years with the Chicago Police Department and twenty years with the Cook County Sheriff's Police, for a total of thirty-one years, it was pure glee, and I could say, "Thanks for the Memories."

Acknowledgement

This book has been developing for years.
It took the peaceful atmosphere of Arkansas
to bring it together.

Thanks go to my wife Penny and our children;
Gina, Steve, Lenny and Susan
for their faith and support.

Also to Sherry Guess for her help.

Section One
Working Midnights

Working Midnights is a different pace.
Crime is very active.
Whenever there was a full moon,
you could expect a wild night.

Many a hospital nurse would call in sick
on the night of a full moon,
since it would usually be
an exceptionally harried evening
for medical people.

Bizarre things just seemed to happen.

Speeding

At the time of this writing, the speed limit on the Eisenhower Expressway, the 'Ike', is 55 mph. I stopped a car doing 85 mph in a 55 mph zone one night. The driver told me he was a doctor going to a suburban hospital.

He said he was in a hurry because his son was injured in an accident and was about to be operated on. He had to get there quickly.

I gave this doctor a pass and asked him to slow down and get to the hospital safely. It was suspicious as the car smelled of booze.

About a year or so later, I stopped a car doing 80 mph in a 55 mph zone. It turned out to be the same doctor, with the same story. The odor of booze was just flowing from the car.

I looked at the doctor and said, "Do you see this ugly face? Have you ever seen it before?

Your story worked about a year ago, but not this time. You're under arrest for DUI." (Driving under the influence).

I sure hope I never need his services with a knife (scalpel) in his hand.

Tony Cuttone

Dumb, and Stupid

While working patrol one day, I received a call for a rape victim. Upon arrival at the 2nd floor apartment, I found a young Hispanic girl naked on the kitchen floor. She was bleeding from her nose and mouth, and her breasts were marked along with her stomach and thighs.

There was no question in my mind that she had been raped. I grabbed a blanket off the bed and covered her. I called for an ambulance to take her to the hospital. I then asked if she knew the man who raped her and she shook her head "No". So I asked her, if a sketch artist drew a picture from her description, would she be able to identify him? She shook her head "Yes" and put her hand to her mouth and lo and behold… took out a piece of her rapist's tongue, about an inch long. She put it in my hand. It was warm and bloody. The ambulance arrived and took her to the hospital.

As fast as I could, I called the radio room and told them to call all the hospitals in the area to watch for any man who comes in with a serious tongue injury. About 10 – 15 minutes later,

I received a call that a man with a serious tongue injury was in the E.R. of a nearby hospital.

Upon arrival at the E.R. and talking with the doctor, I showed him the piece of tongue.

He said, "I can't be 100% sure without an X Ray." I asked the doctor to see if he thought the piece matched without X-rays. He returned and stated "I can't be 100% sure without X-Rays but it looks like a perfect match." I asked if I could go into the room and arrest him. The doctor said "Go ahead, Tony, you've done it many times before."

I went into the exam room where the man was and said only "Hi, amigo, you are under arrest for being dumb and stupid." He responded "I didn't rape that girl." I then said, "Thanks for your confession" and handcuffed him to the cart.

Tony Cuttone

Restroom Please

It was late and I was working on the expressway. I stopped a speeding car on the left shoulder. It was a woman and she was alone in the car. I asked for her driver's license and an insurance card, which she gave me without hesitation. And she then said "I know I was speeding, but I have a problem. I have diarrhea and I am about to soil myself." I started laughing and said "Mrs., I've heard thousands of excuses, but that is the best one I've heard lately. I know you're lying, but I love it!

Here is your license back and get off the next exit and make a right turn and you'll be at a hospital. You can park and go in there and use the restroom.

When she left me, she continued on past the exit I recommended but she wasn't speeding.

Tony Cuttone

Surprise, Surprise!

Traffic at night can be precarious and this event happened to a coworker, Officer Les.

It was in Area 4 Traffic and Les was driving to work. Unexpectedly, he experienced some car trouble. He pulled onto the right shoulder and had the hood of his car up to alert any passersby that his car was stopped. As Les was looking under the hood of the car for the problem, a man came up and said to him, "You've got the front; I'll take the trunk."

Surprise, surprise...Just as the "would-be thief" was about to pop the trunk lock, Officer Les showed his star and a pointed gun. The man was arrested.

Tony Cuttone

Attempted Suicide

Everything seemed to be going well this day until I received a call of a possible attempted suicide. The location was at a second floor apartment in a complex of over 100 apartments built in a circle with a light green garden in the center.

We proceeded to the call at the second floor apartment and when we arrived at the door we could hear a woman crying and screaming. We knocked and a woman opened the door with tears running down her face.

"What's the problem Mrs.?" I asked her.

"My husband is trying to kill himself." She replied.

"Where is he and does he have a weapon, such as a gun or knife?" I asked while looking into the apartment.

"He is in our bedroom", she sobbed, "Down the hall, last door on the right."

We told the woman to sit on the couch quietly and don't come back to the bedroom unless we call you.

We went down the hall to the bedroom, and opened the door. Directly across from the bedroom door were some French doors that opened onto a balcony. On the top metal railing of the balcony was a tied rope coming across the room to our right into a closet. There, standing in the clothes was a man with the rope around his neck. What do you say when you see this?

“What the hell are you doing?” I asked as this man broke from the closet, ran toward the balcony and jumped off!

“Oh shit!”

We ran to the balcony and looked down. He was standing on the grass with the excess rope on the ground and the rope still around his neck looking up. I have been trying for over two years to describe the look on his face. The look said, “WHY AIN’T I DEAD?”

We ran downstairs and grabbed him and put him on the ground. We heard the ambulance coming. My partner, Mike then said “Why don’t we let him go, he won’t get very far.”

The ambulance arrived and he was taken to the hospital for a psych exam and admitted for treatment.

Tony Cuttone

Now, That's a Headache

One night, my partner, Mike and I brought an injured man who was a victim of a strong arm street robbery into the county hospital E.R. One must stop at the police desk and register the person you are bringing into the Emergency Room before you do anything else. We had worked with the police officer at the E.R. desk previously so, after checking on our patient we stopped to chat with this officer for just a minute and grab a cup of coffee.

While talking, he looked over our shoulders at a man walking in. He said "Don't turn Around, you won't believe this one!"

The man came up to the desk asking where he could find a doctor… sticking out of the bridge of his nose was the three-inch handle of a knife, which means the three-inch blade was in his head.

He was asked what his problem was and he said "I've been stabbed." My partner and I started to check his back and his legs, not finding any blood. My partner asked "Where were you stabbed?" The man pointed to his nose. We gave him directions to the men's E.R. and waited. It didn't take long and we heard some nurses screaming loudly.

We tried not to laugh.

Tony Cuttone

Labor Pains

It was a chilly winter evening. Mike and I were assigned to the wagon (prisoner van) and we were sent out to a confinement call 'woman in labor'.

Upon arrival at the second floor apartment, we found a Puerto Rican woman (about 20) naked on the bed with a huge stomach. I asked how far apart the labor pains were. She answered 10 – 15 minutes.

We didn't have 10 -12 hours, but we felt we had time to get her to the hospital. What we did not know was that this was not her first pregnancy. The first thing I did was grab a robe and cover her.

With a straight flight of stairs, my partner and I each had her under the arms and were gently helping her down the stairs. We were almost down the stairs and she froze. She had one leg on the last stair and one leg on the 1st floor landing. She just stopped and told us.

"The baby's coming… the baby's coming!" She didn't budge, so I opened the front of her robe and I could see the baby's head. I started to reach for the baby and the water bag broke and out came the baby, like a Saturn rocket. I grabbed for the baby and I think a finger caught a shoulder. It was so slippery! My partner laid her on the floor and I put the baby on her stomach.

We put her on a cart in the wagon. Mike drove and I calmed the mother in the back with her newborn. I told the mother "You have a beautiful baby girl, do you have a name for her?" She shook her head no, and I said "My wife's name is Penny. Why don't you name her Penny?" with a smile on my face.

We got her to the hospital E.R. and we were in the police room doing our paperwork. An E.R. nurse came in and said, "Well, she did it."

I asked, "Did she have a second one?"

"No. She named the baby Penny."

Somewhere there is a Puerto Rican girl named 'Penny'. My wife was so tickled with the event that she sent a whole bunch of baby girl clothes to her.

Tony Cuttone

Train Accident

There was a train accident on the I.C, (the Illinois Central Commuter) train one early morning. One train rear ended another just south of downtown Chicago. There were many people injured. It was all over the news.

I was assigned to a local hospital to gather information on any passenger brought to the hospital. While sitting in the E.R, a man and woman entered. The man was wearing P.J.'s and the woman had a nightgown and a robe on. They were claiming that they were on the train and were injured. There were no signs of injury on either the man or woman. The radio and TV were reporting this accident constantly.

Trying to control myself from laughing, I took their information and then called for a wagon to transport the couple to the 1st District, which was handling the accident. They both couldn't believe they were being arrested and not being treated for made up injuries.

The only questions I asked after getting their personal data was "Where did you get on the train dressed like you are? You only live 3 blocks from the hospital".

Tony Cuttone

25 Automatic, Do You Have a Concealed Carry Permit for That?

It happened while working nights that Mike and I made a drug arrest of two men and one woman. While we were doing the paperwork, the woman said that she needed the bathroom.

A police woman in the vice unit took the woman to the ladies room and was going to search her before processing.

After a short time, we heard screaming from the toilet.

We raced to the door and we heard the police woman scream, "Get in here to help" which we did. The arrestee was standing there with her slacks and panties around her ankles, and a 25 caliber automatic was on top of her panties on the floor.

The police woman was attempting a strip search, in the normal manner. She had the woman drop her pants, panties and squat.... and out fell a 25 automatic. I picked up the gun and handcuffed the woman which made the policewoman smile and relax. With many arrests a strip search is done and it is legal. The female officer finally put her gun away, which she was holding on the arrestee.

Tony Cuttone

True Love

In the projects in my District, I was assigned to an 'assist citizen'.

Upon arrival, I found a man and his wife in nighttime wear. When I asked what happened, the wife said that her husband had bitten her. There were no marks on her face or arms. She then became insistent that her husband be arrested.

I then had to ask the ridiculous question, "Where did he bite you?"

The woman then opened her robe and nightgown front to show me her breasts. On one breast there was the outline of possible teeth marks. No blood was showing. I started to laugh inside, telling myself I couldn't arrest the husband. So I started to explain to the wife. "What a lucky woman you are to have this man as your husband. You are a very attractive woman with a great body".

She asked, "What do you mean?" I said "Looking at you, I understand he tried to control himself, but couldn't. While trying to get to you, he got carried away while kissing your breast. He tried to arouse you and accidentally bit you, not to hurt you, but…."

The woman was quiet and thought for about a minute, and then went to her husband, put her arms around him and kissed him passionately. I started smiling and said good-bye and got out of the apartment as fast as I could go.

Tony Cuttone

The $100,000 Lie

A very good friend and co-worker, Mark made a traffic stop a little after midnight. A short time later, I heard him say he was arresting a driver on a D.U.I. (drinking and driving).

A day later he was called down to Internal Investigations (I.I.D.). He went there and was told that a complaint had been filed against him.

"What's the complaint?" he asked.

He was told that the man he arrested for DUI stated he owned several gas stations and that there was a gas war going on in the city. This man claimed he had $100,000 in cash in a briefcase in the back seat of his car and now it was missing.

My friend burst out laughing and said "This is a bunch of bullshit! If he had $100,000 in the car, he would be dead now!"

He then walked out of the office and the complaint was deemed unfounded.

The man was trying to kill this DUI by complaining about his 'missing' $100,000. It is just amazing what lies people come up with!

Tony Cuttone

Body Slam

We received a "10-10" call one night, which is *Fight in a Restaurant.* It happened to be a Russian restaurant located in a Shopping Center. This Russian restaurant did not have a liquor license but a customer could bring in some booze, like a bottle of wine or whatever, and drink it at his table.

Quite a few cars responded to the call, knowing that there could be many people involved because of the situation.

Upon arrival, the fight was in the process of spilling out onto the restaurant parking lot.

We were not able to count all the people, but there had to be easily 40 to 50 people involved in the fight.

One of our fellow officers, Fred, was a former W.W.F. (World Wrestling Federation) professional wrestler. He was huge. Fred was injured in a wrestling match. He was hit wrong and he fell wrong, thus injuring his knee. As a result, he was forced to quit the W.W.F. and decided to join the police force where his skills were invaluable.

Fred was walking about 5 feet away from Mike and I. One of the restaurant patrons was walking toward Fred with a bottle in his hand. His face was all scrunched up. I saw this and said to myself, *"Don't try to get Fred!"* The man kept walking toward Fred. He had the bottle raised over his head. When he walked up to Fred, he tried to hit him with the bottle. Big mistake!

Fred blocked the arm with the bottle and picked the man up like he was a piece of tissue paper and then body-slammed him on the asphalt parking lot. The ground shook. You could hear the sound of the body hitting the pavement for quite a distance, I'm sure.

We continued to break up the fighting patrons until peace was restored. If you only had a twisted sense of humor like mine, you'd see the comical action of a drunken man trying to hit a former W.W.F. professional wrestler with a wine bottle and getting body slammed in the parking lot for his trouble.

Tony Cuttone

Teetering

One night about 1:30 a.m., I came upon a car that was balancing on top of the guard rail of a bridge over a major street in Chicago. I stopped behind the car. It was shaking back and forth. I walked up to the driver's side of the car and saw a woman behind the wheel. She was just shaking back and forth. The window was open, so I told the woman, "Sit still, I am here to help you." It was clear she was very frightened.

I had a rope in the trunk of my car and I tied it to the rear axle and to the front end of the squad. I then called for an ambulance and a tow truck. She was terrified, screaming, "help me, help me."

I went back to her car and opened the driver's door of the car. It wasn't damaged.

I told the woman that I was going to get her out. I said, "I'm going to reach up and get your waist in my hands and I want you to put both of your feet to the right of the transmission hump, and on the count of three, I want you to push with both feet and come to the left and I will have you." She agreed.

I reached up and had her by the waist and on the count of three, she pushed with both feet on the right as I pulled on her waist. She came flying out of the car on top of me. I fell back on my back. She was out on top of me on the ground. The woman had a death grip around my neck and wouldn't let go.

The paramedics arrived and they said they couldn't loosen her grip without breaking her hands. They were going to take her to the hospital, with her still on top of me! She knew she was safe now. She kept saying, "thank you, thank you," over and over again but would not let go.

They put me and her on the stretcher and loaded us into the ambulance. They took us to the hospital E.R. The comments from the medical personnel were coming out with laughter and pointing, "Boy, some guys have all the luck."

"What's your secret?"

"You have all the luck in the world!"

After all the comments and all the laughter, the doctor gave the woman a shot and she loosened her death grip and I could finally get up.

This woman was about 40 years old and weighed about 130 pounds.

Tony Cuttone

Businesses

When working in a Police District for a while, you become friendly with many business owners. Such was the case with a wholesale butcher who had whole cattle hanging on hooks in his cooler.

My partner and I were having coffee with this owner and he was telling us about his big phone bills. He complained that he was being billed for many calls to Europe and other countries.

One night when we were working midnights, my partner and I were not on assignment so we were just checking on friends' businesses. We heard some talking and laughing behind the Butcher shop. We stopped the squad, walked behind the building and found six men around the phone box: one talking in a foreign language. After we secured the men, it was found that one was a former phone company repairman. He had gotten together and hooked up a phone to the box and everyone was calling family and friends around the world.

The next day, the owner met with us. My partner and I each received $100 worth of steaks. Several hundred dollars in phone bills were saved by the owner.

Tony Cuttone

The Deserter

One night, a call came in for a '10 – 10' (fight in a tavern). Upon arrival we broke up the fight and had about ten men to arrest.

Then in the station, one of the fighters told me he was in the Army and could I give him a break. I ran his name on the computer, and he came back A.W.O.L. (absent without leave) from Vietnam. I asked him about being A.W.O.L. and he admitted it. He said he worked on a freighter to Canada and came across the border into the U.S.A.

I called the M.P.'s and they responded promptly to the station. They took the man into custody.

About six to eight months later another fight broke out in another tavern and produced the same man, drunk and wanting to fight. Again, I called the M.P.'s and this time their response was, "He is now classified as a Deserter and he will go to jail."

I said, "Good. Take him to jail."

Tony Cuttone

Radio Room

Early, early in the morning, I answered a 911 call in the radio room, and heard a woman crying.

"What's your problem, Mrs.?" I asked.

She responded, "My dog is in labor and is having puppies and she needs help, send the police."

"Mrs., the police do a lot of things above and beyond the line of duty, but we do not deliver puppies. Get your dog to a vet." I replied.

She then thanked me and hung up. I was laughing when I hung up the receiver and told the other police in the radio room. Every one of them volunteered to deliver the puppies just to get out of the Radio Room.

Tony Cuttone

Section Two
Working Days

My wife loved when I worked days.
But getting up at 4:15 a.m. was not always easy.

Once when the alarm went off, all I could do was slide on my knees to the side of the bed. She said my head was buried in the sheets and she thought I was praying. But after ten minutes she didn't think I was praying anymore and called my name.

"Oh, Yah,……I'm up!"

I'm still not a morning person and look back on that time as physically challenging.

One couldn't be late for roll call!

The Professor

The 13th District of Chicago is home to the Puerto Rican mob.

My partner, Mike and I got to know the head of the Latin Kings. He was called "The Professor". The Professor was a straight shooter with Mike and me. The only reason he was called "The Professor" is because he was the only one in the gang who graduated from High School.

One of his orders to the Latin Kings was "Don't hurt any Non-Latin girls."

One night, around 9 p.m., a young Polish boy and girl were walking on Western Avenue, hand in hand, and the Latin Kings jumped them. They both needed to be hospitalized.

That night around 1 a.m., we saw the professor in a fast food joint. We stopped the squad, got out and brought the professor outside. We told him about the young Polish couple and what a bullshitter he was. He claimed that he didn't know anything about it and was going to look into it.

About two or three days later, the professor stopped us and told Mike and I that the three Kings who jumped the Polish couple were now in the hospital, put there by him and the Kings. We thanked him for being a man of his word.

About two years later, the Professor was killed in a gang fight with a rival gang.

Tony Cuttone

Cattle Trespassing/Bovine Breakout

My county area held quite a bit of farmland. One day, while out near the western edge of the county, I received a call saying, "There are cattle in the roadway".

I looked at the radio and said to myself, "Cattle in the roadway; could that be right?" I had never heard a call like that in all my time.

So, I asked the dispatcher if the call was a prank, "Cattle in the Roadway???"

The radio room responded, "That's what we have."

"10 – 4". (Okay) and I drove to the location given on the call.

When I got there, wouldn't you know it, I found nine head of cattle in the roadway!

I asked the dispatcher, "What should I be doing?"

Thankfully, a co-worker came on the air and said, "Turn on the mars lights (rooftop lights) and the cattle will line up and follow you to the farm driveway." Because farmers often feed their cattle from the back of large trucks that move slowly across the field either dropping hay or pellets, cows often adopt the habit of happily following slow moving vehicles.

So, I did that and lo and behold, the cattle got in a column of twos behind the squad and I drove onto the entrance of the farm. The farmer came out and thanked me over and over and said the cattle had once again knocked down some fencing and just went for a nice walk.

We both had to smile over that. He put his cattle behind the fence and thanked me again.

Tony Cuttone

Domestic Battery

I was assigned to an "assist citizen" and a possible battery victim. Upon arrival at the location, the husband and wife met me at the door. The wife's nose was bleeding which tells me that this is a Domestic Battery.

So I asked the couple, "What happened?"

The husband, Andrew, stated that he was sitting on the couch and he demonstrated by going over to sit on the couch. He said he was having a disagreement with his wife.

"She came over to the couch where I was sitting." Andrew said his wife was holding the morning paper and threw the paper at him, hitting him in the head.

While the husband is telling us this story, his wife, Jean walks over to the couch and threw the paper at him. She was swearing at her husband, using some very bad words.

I was just standing there, watching all this and thinking to myself, "*Have they forgotten that the police are here?*"

The husband continued, "She hit me with the paper and I got up." And he did so. He then proceeded to punch her in the face.

I just couldn't believe they were demonstrating exactly what had happened in full force.

I then arrested the husband and said, "You have to be the dumbest S.O.B. I have ever met, hitting your wife in front of me!"

The husband was arrested and charged with simple Domestic Battery.

Tony Cuttone

Barking Dog
Does Your Dog Bite?

It was mid-day when I received this "assist citizen" call. When I arrived at the house, a woman (mother) answered the door and her dog was at her feet barking at me.

On the other side of the room was her teenaged daughter screaming and swearing at the mother.

The barking dog was showing his front teeth and barking relentlessly at me. I asked the mother to put the dog in the bathroom or bedroom and close the door please. The mother kept saying, "Oh, he won't bite! Come on in!"

This went on for several minutes to no avail. I then told the mother, "If that dog bites me, I'll kill it."

She motioned me to come inside and as my left foot went to the threshold, the dog bit me in the left ankle. I drew my gun and shot the dog. It was a small poodle.

The woman started crying and screaming, "You killed my baby, you killed my baby."

The mother/daughter argument was settled and I left the house.

Tony Cuttone

Temporary Divorce

This one couple stands out in my mind as I was frequently going to their house on a Domestic call. I would say I went there more than 20 times.

This man and this woman were meant for each other. They could carry on, disagree and get excited over a can of string beans being turned one way or the other. Go Figure!

There was never any violence between the two of them. And actually, the three of us became friends. Many times the three of us sat in the kitchen, had coffee and I would settle the words between the couple and they'd be lovey-dovey again. It reached a point that when they called the Police, they would ask for me by name.

Then one night, really late they called for me. When I responded to the call, I felt something important had to be done for them. I decided to give them a "temporary divorce."

I had them each put one hand on my star and I divorced them for the night! I sent each one to a separate bedroom for the night with instructions and made them promise that in the morning they would kiss and say good morning to each other. They would have coffee and they would be back to the couple they should be. It worked! I divorced them for the night and in the morning they were married again. They were the nicest people and lived happily ever after.

Tony Cuttone

The Couch

During the King riots across the country and in Chicago where half the city was burning, I ended up working 40 straight hours.

My partner and I were posted in the entrance of a store which was still safe and not yet burning.

We saw a couple with three children come out from a four-story apartment building across the street from us.

A short time later, we saw this husband and wife along with two of their three kids carrying a new couch and the youngest boy had his hands up under it pretending he was helping his parents steal the couch. They carried the new couch into their own apartment building.

Mike and I were just smiling at the sight, knowing that all the stores were just being looted and burned down and in the heat of the rioting, there wasn't much anyone could do to stop it.

Soon the fires reached their apartment building. We then saw the front windows on the third floor burst open and the family pushed the couch out of the window. Thankfully, there was no one on the sidewalk below. When the couch came out of the window, it hit the sidewalk and smashed apart.

The family left the building together and fled for their lives, before their apartment building was consumed by fire.

Tony Cuttone

Democratic Convention

One of the best times with the Chicago Police Department was in the 1960's, during the Democratic Convention in Chicago.

My district was sent to the Chicago downtown area where the Hippies were causing problems, rioting and stealing from the citizens of Chicago. We were taken by bus to Balboa and Wabash Streets. The back of the Conrad Hilton Hotel, which was the Hippie center at that time.

Every policeman was given training on how to use the baton for crowd control. The personnel in my District were lined up to create a human wall between the Hilton and the theatre across from Balboa, probably 150 to 200 policemen in all.

The boss then came up to us and said, "See those lights up there; those are TV lights. No one raise your baton above your head." The response from everyone was "No shit, Dick Tracy."

Right in front of us were several hundred hippies, acting out for the TV cameras. We started moving up the street telling the hippies in front of us to "Get off the street or you may get hurt."

Then all of a sudden, lots of paper bags came flying at us. All seemed to contain animal or human waste (Sh__!).

I didn't get hit, but a bag landed in front of my partner, broke open and brown pieces were all over his pant legs.

That's all. Every policeman started screaming, "Kill, kill" and were charging the hippies, with the batons over our heads.

The hippies started running and knocking each other over. The whole area was the Chicago Loop and the hippies were breaking the store windows and looting the stores.

It was just a wild and crazy time and stopping and controlling the hippies was a big problem. Any persons walking in the Loop were subject to strong arm robbery. No one was safe.

Fighting the hippies went on for about a week. The National Guard had Jeeps with about 6' X 6' of barbed wire mounted on their grill. These Jeeps were used to move and control the hippies.

At that time in Chicago, the Police Department had a unit called the "tough squad", which was used to protect people on Subway and El platforms and also on the streets from robberies. It was also called the "Tuf Squad".

After a period of time, a good week, the hippies moved from Grant Park, in front of the Hilton Hotel, to a Park North at Clark and Diversey. They were having a "War Council" in the park. The sidewalk at the park along Clark Street was lined up with a large number of policemen, shoulder to shoulder, with our backs to the park.

Our Boss came by, stating,: "No one crosses this sidewalk" because the Tuf Squad was going into the park to break up the hippie war council. "If the Mayor and Police Superintendent want to cross the sidewalk into the park, lock their asses up! No one goes into the park, PERIOD!"

Fortunately for all of us, the mayor did not show up. The Tuf Squad went in and broke up the war council of the hippies.

When the Democratic Convention was over and all the members returned home and peace was restored to the City, the mayor held a press conference on TV. The Governor at the time was a former U.S. Attorney in Chicago. He called the confrontation a "police riot". The mayor did everything to control himself from telling the Governor what he thought of him. He ended his speech, with what I believe is the best speech I have ever heard or will ever hear.

"I want to thank the police Department and others for protecting the citizens of Chicago and the members of the convention. They did such a great job against high odds, that I am giving each and every one of them a $5,000 raise."

Could you ever hear a better speech than that if you were a Chicago policeman? I doubt it!

Tony Cuttone

No One Enters

One day at roll call, while working days, the Boss asked me to take a recruit under my wing. His Training Officer had called in sick and at one time, I had been a training officer. I agreed to take the recruit for that day.

Assigned to a 'man shot' call, we arrived at the scene to find a man shot and he was dead. I called for paramedics and the crime lab. The room was a mess; chairs and tables knocked over and blood everywhere. Procedure dictates that the crime scene be left untouched until the crime lab arrives.

I stationed the recruit at the front door and told him, "No one comes in except the crime lab or medics," and to call me so that I could have them walk in without disturbing evidence until pictures were taken, etc.

It so happened that the DC (District Commander) was on the street, going to or coming back from lunch. He stopped at the crime scene. When he came to the door, the recruit stopped the DC from coming into the apartment. He told the recruit who he was and that he wanted to come in. The recruit then told the DC that if he tried to enter his "ass would be locked up." The DC then left the area.

The next day, the DC complimented me on training the recruit, because we were both right.

Tony Cuttone

Cards

While working Vice in the District, my partner and I were friends with a man who owned a store on a side street. He couldn't rent the place so he and about 15 - 20 of his friends would gather together and play cards there.

We called these guys "the old timers" as the youngest of them was about 100 years old.

The old guys would meet three days a week in the store for their card games. They would play poker, gin rummy, canasta and whatever else. One of the old timers' wives would cook a lunch for the guys. My partner and I had an open invitation to join them for lunch.

The store windows were blacked up and no one could look into the store from the sidewalk. This old timer's club was just a nice bunch of guys, never hurting anyone.

One day the boss of the Vice Unit had a meeting in the morning. He told us all that we were going on a raid for illegal gambling. Guess where?... the old timer's club.

The boss would not listen to us telling him it was a group of old timers having fun. There was nothing organized about them.

I left the station and went to an outside pay phone and called the club house. I told them we would be there between 12:30 and 1 p.m. They could play cards but have no money showing on the tables. I asked: "Do you understand what I'm telling you?"

"No money showing on the tables. Yeah, yeah. We understand. Thanks a lot."

The time came and we went on the raid. We walked into the club and there were 17 old timers playing various card games and low and behold, money showing on all the tables.

My partner and I couldn't believe it.

All 17 had to be arrested, so the boss said. I pulled the owner to the side and gave him a little bit of hell. "Didn't you understand me when I called you?" He just smiled at me and said nothing.

Everyone was brought into the lock-up. Our friend asked if he could use the phone to call his wife. I said yes and brought him to a desk with a phone so he could call his wife, which he did.

"Those dirty S.O.B.'s Tony and Mike arrested all of us for nothing. Go to the bank and bring me some bond money." He said.

I would never do it, but I wanted to hit him. He was smiling and then he began to laugh. He said his wife couldn't get to the bank until the morning. Then I started to laugh and I called him every swear word I could think of. For him and his friends, this was a big adventure. I ended up posting his bond and driving him home. We were friends forever.

Tony Cuttone

It's a Secret

Back in the 60's, during the Puerto Rican Riots, my partner and I were working days. We were on North Avenue when a call came in, "Shooting at the police; 1300 Leavitt."

We were just three blocks away from the scene and drove right there with no lights or siren going. We got to the area and could not see a single policeman. Just then, a bullet came screaming through the windshield and into the back rest of the front seat between Mike and myself. We told the radio room it was a trap and no policemen were in the area.

I myself was really scared. In fact I was so scared, I wet myself. I started to drive to the District station to change my uniform pants. I had an extra pair of pants in my locker. I looked at Mike and said, "Don't tell anyone what just happened to me, because if you do, I will get even with you, even though we are good friends, and we have saved each other's ass before."

He looked at me and said, "Don't worry. Don't you tell anyone that I just shit my pants. Neither one of us told anyone anything. We kept each other's secret to this day. And we were both laughing.

Tony Cuttone

Poor Mink Coat

It was a cold wintry night and I was on the Midnight shift. I came to a stoplight at Ashland and North Avenue. There was a car stopped on my right at the red light. Then a car skidded into the rear of the car on my right. I turned on the mars lights and got out of the squad. There was not much damage on either car. The 2nd car had skidded on the slippery street.

The driver of that car was a young guy about 18 years old. He was behind the wheel of his car, the driver's window was open and the smell of booze was flowing from the car.

The driver was drunk and he was drooling from his mouth onto his shirt and pants. I took him out of the car and told him he was under arrest for DUI. He gave me his Driver's License and insurance card. I put him in the rear seat of the squad and then walked up to the driver of the front car and he was just as mad as he could be.

He was swearing at the boy who rear-ended him. There were no broken taillights on his car, just a dent in the bumper. Low and behold, the right door of the car was open and the wife was lying in the street gutter with a full length mink coat on. She was lying on the melted snow, rock salt and dirt. I shook my head. There was not enough impact from the accident to force the door open. She had to have opened the door herself and laid down in the gutter. I immediately knew how phony this was and I had to play their game. I told the husband that the boy did not have insurance on his car, just a stretch of the truth for the situation. He again went off like a Saturn rocket;

screaming and swearing. He then called to his wife, “Selda, get up, the S.O.B. doesn’t have any insurance!”

His wife got up from the gutter with all kinds of dirt and “gunk” dripping from her mink coat. It probably cost a bundle to have it cleaned and treated.

I gave the man a copy of the accident report which showed the insurance info, but I didn’t point it out to him. I then sent the couple on their way, wishing them the best.

The boy was taken in to the station and arrested for DUI. He was tested, showing that he was drunk. While doing the paperwork, the boy just wouldn’t stop swearing at me. “You dirty, f_ _ ing cop. You’re a M.F.” So, in order to help him calm down I handcuffed him to the radiator and told him, “Little boy, stop swearing.” Then he was put in a cell.

In court, his license was suspended for a year.

Tony Cuttone

K.K.K.

A co-worker was in a fight and he was I.U.D. (injured on duty) with a back injury. He lived in the country outside the city and used a walker.

One day while he was at home recovering, the doorbell rang. When he opened the door it happened to be the K.K.K. looking for donations (money). He wasn't going to give them any money, but he asked them to wait and he went to a closet and took a half box of 38 caliber shells.

The two K.K.K. members jumped for joy, thanking him for the bullets.

The next night, the K.K.K. returned with gifts, including a cake for him, hoping he would join the K.K.K. and probably become their leader.

He didn't join the K.K.K.

Tony Cuttone

Section 3

The preceding stories have all been written by Retired Police Officer, Anthony (Tony) Cuttone.

Have you picked your favorite?

The following humorous stories come from fellow Officers around the country. We would like to thank them for their contribution:

Enjoy!

To Protect & Serve *Does That Include Doing Laundry?*

Individuals are drawn to Law Enforcement for different reasons. Some because they had a family member that they grew up admiring. Some because it is a noble profession that allows you to help others and thereby receive great personal satisfaction internally, while many others like the idea of not having to look forward to doing the same old thing each day, day in and day out, year after boring year. Contrary to this last belief, there are constants even in the unpredictable world of Law Enforcement. This is my story about one of those days and events.

I was just beginning my shift when a Sergeant friend of mine named Mike asked if he could tag along. I was a new Sergeant and I needed to pick the experienced brain of my friend every chance I got. I always enjoyed Mike's company, so I told him to hop in and we were off.

I was working the four to midnight shift and it was the middle of the week so I wasn't expecting too much especially since Mike and his crew had been so busy that same day. I say that because we were a mid-sized city and usually, if one shift was busy, then the next shift would be slow. It was one of those "Murphy's Law" things that seemed to run true most of the time. Law Enforcement is unpredictable in many ways but in other ways, it isn't. Just like the sun will rise in the east and set in the west and what goes up must come down…yes, there are constants in Police work. It would not be long before Mike and I would be given our first "regular" call for the day.

It was 6:11 p.m. when the dispatcher called my unit and advised us of a 'Domestic Disturbance' at a house number we were all too familiar with. Remember those constants I was telling you about? Well, as long as there are husbands and wives working hard to make a living, there will be couples coming home and fighting. Bad day at work, a couple of beers or drinks and they are ready to let loose! We looked at it as job security because as long as we had families like this in our city we would have a job going to their house to help keep the peace. Every week at least once we would be sent to help them get along. Most of the time it was just talking and warning and they were good for the night. Other times, an arrest was necessary and guess who was up there before us, ready to bail their loved one out... yep, the spouse they were arguing with minutes before. Prior to this call, Mike and I had been talking about the usual things cops talk about. Low pay, politics, and leadership in the Department we worked for, etc.

That all changed after this call and we began to discuss the stupidity of answering so many calls to the same address. We challenged each other on what we had done in the past and the things we had tried to solve this reoccurring irritation. Nothing had worked. Suggestions of help from their Church or counseling from other professionals, arrests, fines, all had failed. Was there anything we could do to break the cycle this poor couple was in? Together on this evening we challenged each other to give it another try.

At the scene it was just as we had suspected. Same old, same old. Came home from work, drinking then arguing and finally the call to the police Dispatcher to send a car. Also, there was the always, “he started it, No! she started it” deadlock. This was the drama of their world and each week either myself or some other poor cop had to deal with it. Don’t get me wrong, we feel for the families that live this way and want to help, but too often they will not listen to good advice and arguing becomes the “norm”.

So, there we were again, trying to talk to them and both angry, saying the other was to blame and started the whole mess. We were just about to leave and had let the wife go to the back rooms while we spoke to the husband with one last plea to get along or stay away from each other for the rest of the evening. He was in his recliner and facing the TV, already tuning into the program and tuning us out when he said something in frustration that gave us hope. What he said was, “as soon as you leave, she’ll just start in on me again!” That’s it! We’ll just wait in the next room and watch and when she thinks we’ve left, she’ll come out and we will see firsthand that she’s the guilty party who’s starting the arguments. It was flawless. Why hadn’t we thought of this before” She was in the far end of the house where the bedrooms were at. Her husband was in the living room and just past that on the other end of the house was the kitchen and the laundry room.

We told the husband not to say a word or to do anything to provoke her. We hid just inside the kitchen with the lights out and waited. In our excitement, we should have paid more attention to what was going on in the laundry room behind us. The wife had been washing clothes and we didn't even notice it until the washing machine stopped and the house got quieter. After the machine stopped, here comes the wife! From the back rooms down the hall, we saw her walking toward the living room where her husband was quietly watching TV. We got her now, I thought. Then the perfect plan blew up in our faces. She never even looked at her husband, but walked right on by him heading for the kitchen. We panicked and headed toward the closest room we could get to and that was the laundry room. Most laundry rooms are not that big and this one was no exception. The only place to hide was behind the laundry room door and Mike quickly took that spot. Hoping for a miracle that she only needed something out of the kitchen, I placed myself in front of the washing machine, praying that she wouldn't see me. God must have been amused watching us because He didn't bail me out of this one. The wife never stopped in the kitchen but headed straight for the laundry room. Cops will tell you it's amazing sometimes how quickly your mind works under pressure. I realized she was there to check on the washing machine that I, as well as she, heard stop just a few minutes before. I, to this day don't know why I did what I did, but as she walked into the laundry room I lifted the lid to the washing machine, handed her some wet clothes as I separated them like you're supposed to do and began talking about little things like how long they had lived in the house and what a nice home they had. Behind the door I could hear Mike trying not to laugh. She never questioned why I was still in her house and still in her laundry room.

Mike said it was the funniest thing he had seen in years and couldn't believe how cool I acted under the circumstances. I never told him how shook I really was and embarrassed about the whole deal.

It ended with me helping her put the clothes in the dryer and then she left me and headed back toward the back of the house again. I was never as relieved in my life as I was to get out of that house and back in to my squad car. Of course, Mike laughed the rest of the night and probably still tells the story of how we responded to a domestic call and ended up doing their laundry. Oh well, I told him that evening, our motto is to protect and SERVE. "Yeah," said Mike, "but does that include laundry?"

Courtroom Scene
Unexpected Birthday Present

There can be a thin line between humor and irony, so let's explore a Court Room situation.

It was the first case of the day; that of a young man who had many offenses with a bad attitude.

You never know which judge you'll have in court and today was a particularly tough judge. Both sides were presented, and the young man, Sam, was snickering the whole time.

After all the evidence had been presented, the judge was ready to pronounce sentence. The judge asked Sam, "Do you have anything to say before I pronounce sentence?"

Sam replied, in a surly voice, "yea, it's my birthday."

At that point, the judge stood up and sang,

"Happy Birthday to you, Happy Birthday to you, Five Years in Vandalia (State Prison), Happy Birthday to you."

The court Room went into hysterics and the officers removed Sam from the courtroom.

Sarg'

Just a Minute

Officer Jack was making a traffic stop. It so happened that the driver was someone that he knew and said that he was looking for his brother. The blue lights on his squad are going round and round as he approached the car. He knocked on the drivers' window.

Nothing happened … He cleared his throat loudly…Nothing happened.

The driver had his head down and was looking at the passenger.

Officer Jack went to the passenger's side of the car. The passenger was smoking a joint and rolling another.

Officer Jack asked, "What are you doing?"

The passenger said, "Just a minute" and attempted to throw the joint out the window but the window was closed and it came right back on himself.

The driver exclaimed, "Dude! … Busted!

He was so stoned….

Drug Bust

Whenever the conversational pleasantries seem too nice, that's a clue that there's probably more here than meets the eye.

Officer Andy stopped a weaving car and saw a rolled joint above the driver's ear.

So he asked, "Do you smoke marijuana?"

"Not really, man." said the driver.

The officer said, "So what's that above your ear?"

The driver touched the weed, made a sad face and nonchalantly said, "Oh, I forgot about that."

So, Officer Andy said, "Do you have any more?"

"Sure, man" replied the offender. "Look here" and showed a whole pocketful of the stuff.

With widening eyes, the officer asked again, "Do you have any more?" and heard…

"Sure do!" and another pocketful of weed appeared. He was so polite and SO buzzed!

Opossum

Officer Chris has had many calls involving animals. One of his favorite calls was, "Help! There's an opossum on my porch! This animal is so scary! Send the police! I need an Officer right away!"

"Now, now, that opossum is just probably enjoying the scenery," Said Officer Chris.

"He'll go away soon." We called this local caller "King Possum.

Chocolates

Forrest Gump said "Life is like a box of Chocolates... You never know what you're going to get."

Officer Chris said that's how police work frequently was for him.

I went on a call of 'Illegal Trash Dumping'" at the Marina.

When I got to the door, I knocked and heard, 'Come In', so in I went."

There was a woman smoking a joint and rolling another.

Don't you think one should see who's at the door before you invite them in to view objectionable behavior? pondered Officer Chris.

Sergeant Waring

Ghost Call

Every couple of months, we get a new rash of this type of call. And it is always from educated, well respected people. They swear that there are ghosts in their home.

In this case, Officer Chris responded to the call from an elderly male resident who stated that he was seeing some sort of apparitions in his home.

This resident lost his spouse the year before and I was there at that call. The resident seemed to have all his faculties and was not impaired in any way. He told me he had been seeing "people" in his home for the past year or so and it had been unsettling to him.

He told me in great detail some of the dealings with these apparitions. He told me that these "people" were not threatening and did not speak. Many of them wore strange hats and moved objects in his house. He told me that recently he made the bed and when he went back into the bedroom, he saw one of the "people" get into the bed and pull up the covers. Together, we went room-to-room and checked the house completely and found nothing. The resident was very sincere and told me he was not crazy. While at the residence, he thought he saw one of the "people" get into my patrol vehicle and put on my hat. I looked and saw nothing, however he had no way of knowing my hat was inside the vehicle.

The resident told me when I pulled into his driveway the "people" disappeared. I told the resident I believed him and did not think he was crazy. The resident previously had the locks changed on his house since this started happening about a year ago. The "people" appeared as normal people, not translucent like a ghost. The resident told me that he and his wife both saw "people" at the same time once. I asked him if he was the only owner of the house and he said no, but he would check on that and learn more about the history of his home.

I suggested if this continued, he might want to consult with a company that deals with the paranormal. I was thanked for my time and I resumed patrol.

Sergeant Waring

House Shaking

The mysterious shaking house was another memorable call that Officer Chris responded to. The homeowner stated that there was a strange vibration that shook her entire house. She had reported this three times in the last two years and wanted something done.

She told me that at 7:00 a.m. that same morning, she awoke to a feeling of the entire bed vibrating. Of course, she wanted me to lie on her bed as that was the only way she said I could feel the vibrations. I politely declined.

After she got up that morning, she found her dryer had seized up and her hot water was not working to her washing machine, however the hot water was working throughout the rest of the home.

The homeowner told me that she believed one of her neighbors was causing the problem by operating a treadmill. She was certain of this because all three homes were built on the same piece of rock, and she was sure the vibrations were carrying over to her residence. To resolve the problem, she had the roof replaced twice and still the problem persisted. She was unable to afford any additional repairs and wanted me to resolve the problem immediately.

I spoke with the other residents and they said they could feel nothing unusual and were not operating any machines that could cause the vibrations described. I suggested that she call a repairman to check her washer and dryer and maybe look under the house to see if anything seemed amiss.

She was not happy with my suggestion and wanted to talk to the chief of police. I advised her of his hours for her convenience. She assured me that she had recently been to a doctor and was told she was not crazy, but was actually in good health.

She claimed that the last law officer to come over told her this was either her body having the shakes or it was all in her mind. Clearly unable to resolve the problem, I excused myself and resumed patrol.

Sergeant Waring

It's a Bomb!

Detective David shares a call:

I was investigating a rape and as part of the investigation, a search warrant was executed on the suspect's residence. The suspect was a self-described "survivalist" who was convinced that the government would someday fall and anarchy would be the rule of the day.

The suspect had numerous weapons and ammunition caches throughout his property, as well as piles of gear and supplies. One of our biggest fears was that the suspect had placed explosives and booby traps around his residence, so I cautioned all of the officers to stop and report if they discovered anything that looked suspicious, and not to touch or move any suspected explosives they discovered. A bomb squad was on call, but was several hours away, so a decision to proceed had been made.

As the search of the residence began, officers did find several small items of explosive material, such as blasting caps and uncompleted pipe bombs. This raised the officers' level of concern as each officer searched a different area.

One of the officers was searching a clothes dresser and suddenly yelled out "Bomb!" I immediately cleared the area of all the other officers.

As the rest of the officers restlessly waited outside with great concern, I approached the dresser to observe what the device looked like and to try and get whatever information that I could to relay to the bomb technicians.

I saw what the officer had seen, a clear acrylic cover with multi colored wires inside. You could see a battery and some electronics inside, and several small led lights that had begun to flash. As the "device" began flashing, a small noise came from the drawer and some of the clothing slowly fell away from this deadly explosive.

What I then observed was a "personal" vibrator! It was in the "usual shape" but that could not be seen until the clothing was removed to make it obvious what it was.

Apparently, as the officer looked inside the dresser drawer, he had inadvertently hit the "on" button.

Needless to say, that officer was mercilessly ribbed about his bomb.

Detective David

Don't Shoot

Officer Bill was walking his beat. It was a cool fall night. Everything seemed quiet. He was checking the back doors of the businesses to be sure they were secure. There were some empty boxes and cartons behind the stores, so he gave each one a shake. But one didn't budge.

He raised his gun and said, "I'll count to three and then I'll fire a round into this box!"

"No! Don't shoot!" replied a squeaky voice. And out tiptoed a little black boy!

Off to the police station they marched. The boy said he didn't know his address but he knew where his house was. They walked awhile and finally went to the location that the boy thought was his house. By now it was 3 am. Officer Bill rang the doorbell and a white man came to the door. Officer Bill asked, "Is this your son?"

The man stared at the boy and then looked at Officer Bill and said, "You must be joking!" with astonishment in his voice.

So back to the police station we marched. The officer never knew the final outcome.

Officer Bill McElwain

Saturday Night

It was a Saturday Night and Officer Bill was dispatched to the American Legion Post.

There was a lady there who had some lumps, obviously put there by her husband.

She did not want to sign a complaint. In fact, she asked if we would go check on him and make sure that he got home okay.

First mistake…we agreed.

When we arrived at the house, we rang the doorbell. An elderly lady answered the door and we could see three children in a room off to the left. I asked if the subject was home. She said yes and that he had just gone up the stairs.

I looked at the staircase and the subject was coming down the stairs loading a 12 gauge pump shotgun. I tried the screen door and found it locked. He came over to the screen door and jacked a shell into the chamber. He was pointing the weapon at me.

We could have killed him then, but I made a quick decision that the booze was talking for him. I told him that his wife had asked us to check and be sure that he got home okay.

He said, "Well, I am home. Now get off my f—ing porch."

We complied.

Upon returning to the station, the captain wanted to know what happened. We told him and he said, "Get the car. We're going to get the S.O.B."

I said, “We can’t do that, Cap. There are children and an old lady in there. We will get him later.”

The next Saturday night, a call came into the station that there was a car at the Mulberry St. crossing of the CB & Q RR (Chicago, Burlington and Quincy Railroad) with the driver slumped over the wheel. It was that same guy from the previous Saturday night. He went to jail.

The next morning, he was screaming and yelling in the lock-up! I went back to see what his problem was. He was told that the charge was ‘Intoxicated on a Public Highway’. He was also reminded of the previous Saturday night incident.

He said, “Oh, I was just kidding with a shell in the chamber.”

Officer Bill McElwain

Lumber Yard

A citizen who lived next door to a lumber yard called the station to inform the police that the lumber yard office had been broken into.

Officer Bill and his partner, Kenny got the call. Upon arrival, Kenny met the owner and entered the Lumber yard office through the broken door.

In a matter of seconds, the suspect jumped through the plate glass insert in the front door and landed on the sidewalk. At that moment, a car slowly approached the scene. My first thought was, *"Uh, Oh! Here come his pals."*

As I was turning to keep the subject and the car in my view, I noticed that the subject was apparently trying to rush me. I fired a round at him that missed as he ran down alongside the lumber yard in the dark.

I fired two more rounds in rapid succession that hit him. The subject took off running for two blocks where another squad apprehended him. His wife, who was with him was also arrested.

Officer Bill McElwain

Warrant

We were called into the station at 4 a.m. Upon arriving, the desk sergeant informed my partner and me that the Captain wanted to see us.

Upon entering the Skipper's office, we were informed that he had information that a subject wanted on a felony warrant was at home and he handed us the warrant to serve.

When we arrived at the subject's home, we were informed by his mother that he was home. At that moment he appeared in the hallway in night clothes.

Mistake #1. Subject asked to go to his bedroom to change into street attire. We said, "Okay." I followed him to his second floor bedroom. He went and stood by a piece of furniture with drawers. I unstrapped my revolver in the event that he would reach in the drawer and come up with a weapon.

I could see that he thought better of it and went out into the hallway. There, I lost sight of him for a matter of seconds.

Then, I heard glass crashing and I determined that he had jumped through a second floor window in an attempt to flee an arrest.

I ran down the stairs and informed my partner of what had happened. My partner went out in the back of the house and I went to the front.

I heard my partner yell, "Halt!" and then a shot was fired, then another shot.

The subject then yelled, “Don’t shoot again, I’m hit.”

At that time, we took him into custody and transported him to the E.R. of St. Mary’s Hospital where he was patched up and taken to jail from there.

Officer Bill McElwain

Dumb as a Box of Hammers

We had been dealing with a young man for years, first as a juvenile, and later as an adult.

This young man could not keep from stealing and the thought never entered his head that he could get an honest job and buy what he needed instead of stealing things.

This young thief would take some of the dumbest things, leaving far more valuable items behind.

Most of the items he took were immediate needs or wants, such as food, clothing or a pair of especially nice sneakers, etc.

One summer day, the temperature had become extremely hot. A theft was reported at one of the local stores, which was located in a very rural area of the county. The only items reported stolen were a gallon of ice cream and some soda pop.

As Deputies responded to the area, one of the Deputies noticed this young man walking along the side of the highway eating ice cream from a gallon container. The Deputy stopped and spoke to the man and he admitted that he had taken the items because he was hot and thirsty.

The Deputy arrested the young man and searched his pockets. In one pant pocket the Deputy discovered a small bag of marijuana. The young man looked at it in amazement and stated that it was not his, because he had just stolen the pants from a house up the road.

Detective David

Snakes

One morning I was sent to investigate a possible suicide at a residence in the county. I arrived to discover that the resident had, in fact, shot himself and was deceased.

As part of the investigation, I was searching the residence for any evidence that may explain the death of this man. The man lived by himself, and I noticed a large number of cricket and mouse cages in the house that were being used to raise these animals and insects.

As I looked through the residence, I was becoming very uncomfortable. There were a large number of reptile books and magazines in every room. I am deathly afraid of snakes and will avoid them at almost any cost.

Additional investigators were nearby and came over to assist me as I searched the house and documented the scene.

The entire residence was searched except for one room which I saved for last. As I entered the room, with the other investigators following, I noticed that two whole walls were covered with sheets. The room was very hot and humid, and there were lights behind the sheets illuminating some type of cages that completely covered both walls.

With great trepidation, I slowly pulled back the sheets and discovered all the cages contained either large lizards or were filled with snakes of different colors.

The other investigators, knowing my intense fear of snakes, were making comments about the snakes escaping after finding one cage door ajar. They were delighted to watch me fidget and look with wide eyes at the slithering mess of reptiles.

One of the investigators, who was standing next to me, slowly ran his shoe tip up the back of my leg. Without bothering to look at what had touched me, I let out a blood curdling scream and broke for the door, pulling my pistol as I ran from the room.

All of the other investigators were laughing up to that point. Once the gun cleared the holster, they also took off running, not from the snakes, but from me. I think at that moment, they realized that there was a very real threat of being injured and that their little joke had backfired.

It Ain't Me

Around 1995 while processing a person that I had arrested at the Police Station, I heard a pursuit start that was headed South on I-40 toward Little Rock. The pursuit lasted long enough that I finished booking my prisoner just as the suspect was returning through a nearby town, Conway.

I left the station and joined the pursuit. After about another 80 miles, the suspect missed a turn and ran off the road. He fled on foot into a farm field. I eventually found him, face down in the mud.

When I focused my flashlight on him he looked up and said, "Officer, it ain't me."

Later, I learned that he meant that the drugs made him do it!

Bill Milburn

Soul Night

As Sergeant on the Street Crimes unit, I got to be creative. The local skating rink had what they called "Soul Night" on Sunday nights.

The normal practice was to go to a local convenience store afterwards and carry a large amount of food and drink into the restroom. They would leave a lookout and when the police arrived, everyone would drop what they had not consumed on the floor and there was no way to positively identify who had stolen what.

After about the third week, I developed a plan. I found a large box and placed it in a toilet stall and wrote out of order on the box. About 30 minutes before the normal arrival time of the shoplifters, I got in the box in which I had poked a small peep hole. As usual, the group came in, stole a quantity of food and drink and came into the restroom. I watched long enough to identify who I thought was the leader.

At just the right time, I kicked the box over and was standing in the middle of them in full uniform. The leader ran out the door and I tackled and cuffed him in the middle of the store. As the crowd gathered around, I told them that I would be there next week. I said I may be in the air vent or I may be in the freezer but I would be there. That ended the problem and they never came back.

Bill Milburn

New Year's Eve

Around 1990, on New Year's Eve, I was working the DWI Task Force. I made a traffic stop on a well-endowed co-ed in a low cut evening gown.

After performing all the normal field sobriety tests, I arrested her and transported her to the Police Department to run a "Breath Test".

Her case came to court on a day when one of the fifth grade classes from the public schools was attending court. They all sat in the front two rows. After I finished testifying as to what led up to the roadside arrest, the prosecutor asked me if I performed any additional tests at the station. I stated that after arriving at the station, I had performed a "Breast Test".

The fifth grade class erupted in laughter, rolling in the floor. The Judge turned red and immediately took a recess. After the Judge had time to settle himself down, he resumed court. He was still so flustered that he found her "Guilty of Driving while in violation of the Arkansas Hot Check Law."

Bill Milburn

Dog Man

Despite all the training and practice that takes place for critical situations, sometimes an Officer will have a really stupid moment. One time in particular was during the execution of a Search Warrant.

We had a drug house under surveillance for several weeks. We noted large drug sales and also that weapons were present and in reach of the bad guy. We knew that the person we had been watching had a large dog inside the residence, and noted over several weeks that the dog had a bad disposition. People going into the residence to buy drugs had to be very careful while they were around that dog.

When we served our warrant, we had an Officer detailed to go in with the entry team. His sole job was to get between the dog and the Officers and, if necessary, to kill the dog if it began to threaten or bite the Officers. We called him our "dog man".

When the time came for the warrant to be served, the "dog man" was supposed to be the third person into the residence, in a line of seven. Instead, he fell back and was the seventh man in.

As we entered the residence, we secured each room, placing each person found inside on the ground and handcuffing them. Our suspect ran into a back room where both drugs and weapons were located.

As I raced after him, the dog jumped up from behind the couch and bit my leg at the calf.

The dog would not turn loose and, since it was a big dog, I could hardly run and drag it along. I could not shoot it because it was attached to my leg and there were children in the room that I was in.

I saw two more Officers behind me and directed them to secure the suspect in the next room. I yelled for someone to help me get the dog to stop biting me and saw the "dog man" walking towards me pointing a shotgun at the dog.

I immediately yelled at him to not shoot, since the dog was attached to my leg by his teeth and the dog was between me and the "dog man". The "dog man" had a wild look in his eyes and I realized that he was so focused on the dog, he had developed "tunnel vision" and probably did not even see me, just the dog.

I had one of those "Oh, God, if you will just help me this once…" moments, picturing this idiot Officer shooting the dog and me.

At that point, thankfully, the dog turned loose and backed up. I was able to grab the "dog man" and keep him from shooting the dog, me and anything else.

Needless to say, we had a successful search, a bad bite, and the next day, transferred the "dog man" off the entry team.

Alien Probe

Every officer gets his share of calls that deal with less than completely stable individuals.

I think all Officers dread these calls because you never know what will happen. You do wind up responding to many of these same people over and over again.

I was sent on one call concerning a very odd gentleman. He was always hearing voices outside his house and was convinced that someone was trying to make him go crazy.

I had been to this house on the same complaint every night for almost a week. The man lived in a very rural area and there were no neighbors for almost a mile in any direction.

After having listened to the man tell me about his "alien probe" experiences, it did not take a rocket scientist to figure out that this was a disturbed individual.

On this night, I decided that I was sick and tired of coming out to the middle of nowhere, in the middle of the night to look for non-existent people outside his house.

When I got there, I spoke with the man and told him I would look around outside and asked him to wait on the front porch. I walked behind the house and shined my flashlight.

All I could see were deer grazing well out in a pasture. Once again, no one was there and the only voices that he heard were inside his head.

I stopped behind the house and screamed for the imaginary people to stop and put their hands up. I then drew my pistol and fired three rounds into the ground.

When I came back to the front of the house, the man was wide eyed. I explained that the people ran off and would probably never be back. The man nodded vigorously and went back into his house.

I did not get another call to that residence for three or four months, and that was so he could tell me that he had not heard a thing and decided to move.

Moving Pencil

One of the loudest 911 calls Officer Chris ever responded to included six screaming women at a country club.

We were called to the country club and told there was a large rattle snake inside the building. This could be a life threatening situation and when I arrived at the scene, the fire chief offered to help me with the call.

Grateful for his assistance, as we entered the area, we found six women huddled in the corner and a five-gallon bucket over "the snake". I began to slide the bucket carefully, knowing if I were bitten, it could be deadly, but it felt empty and while slowly sliding the bucket across the floor, it caught on a tile and the bucket tipped over. The women began to shreek as the serpent was now loose.

The fire chief and I managed to subdue a six inch long, harmless grass snake that was no larger than an average pencil. We took the dangerous serpent to the nearby woods and released it, knowing the snake was probably very stressed from all the screaming it had endured while under the bucket.

Sergeant Waring

So, You Think You're Smart

We executed a Search Warrant at the residence of a man that had been selling drugs for some time. He had already been arrested twice for selling controlled substances, and had gone to prison once. He was currently out on bond for the same thing.

When we entered the residence, he was in his bedroom. He ran to the adjoining bathroom and we heard the commode flush before we could get the door open and place him in custody.

He was quite proud of himself for flushing all of his drugs and getting rid of the evidence. He was all smiles and snide comments.

Imagine his surprise when one of the Officers walked out of the bathroom with a glass container with around two ounces of methamphetamine inside and a cork lid.

The Officer grinned at the man and calmly told him that next time he flushed his drugs, make sure he kept them in a container that did not float.

The man just turned pale and deflated. With the most pitiful voice, he confessed to all of the drugs and even told us where other smaller amounts were that we had not yet found.

He was well and truly broken.

Goats

There are a lot of times that we, as Law Enforcement Officers, subject our bodies to abuse. Whether having to chase someone and falling down, or on the ground trying to subdue and arrest someone.

What many people do not understand is that our clothes take a greater degree of punishment than we do sometimes.

I had gone on a call to do a welfare check on an elderly lady who had been sick. Her family could not reach her by phone, and had asked if an Officer could go out to her house and check on her.

When I arrived, I discovered that the lady was sitting on her porch enjoying a beautiful day. I stood by the porch and visited with her for several minutes, while her two goats came up to me and sniffed my shoes. One of the goats kept pulling on my pant leg down by my boot top. I would try to push the goat away, but it just kept nibbling and tugging at my pant leg.

After a couple of minutes of this, it was getting old and the tugs were getting more insistent. Finally the goat got a full mouthful of my pant leg and yanked its head back, tearing a fist sized chunk of my pants off.

I yelled at the goat and tried to kick at it, which seemed to infuriate the lady. Next thing I knew, the lady, who had moments before been thanking me for checking on her, was yelling at me and telling me not to hurt her goats.

I could only shake my head and get back in my vehicle. I guess the lady would have been perfectly content to watch her goats pick me clean. This all would have been funny except I had to buy a new pair of pants.

Motorcycle Cop

While on traffic patrol on S.I.H. 35 without radar on my motorcycle, I sat up on an overpass, where I would not be observed watching the traffic flow.

I observed an 18 wheeler tailgating and swerving in the lanes back and forth. I accelerated my motorcycle down an 'On" ramp, falling in behind said 18 wheeler, and followed long enough to pace said vehicle at 80 mph.

I turned on my front red lights and positioned myself as to be seen by the semi driver but to no avail. Same speed of 80 m.p.h. was continued with the changing of lanes back and forth with me following behind. Tired of this, I turned on my siren but again, no response. Finally, I pulled up to the driver in the lane to his left and observed him talking on his C.B. while I kept tapping my siren.

Finally he looked to his left and saw me. I signaled for him to pull over while I observed his mouth uttering "Oh, shit".

After the 18 wheeler was able to pull over and stop on the right shoulder of the expressway, I dismounted my motorcycle and approached the driver. The first thing out of his mouth was "Why are you stopping me?"

I asked him to step down from his cab which he did. Again he asked, "Why are you stopping me?"

I responded for speeding, tailgating, unsafe lane change and driver inattention.

He asked, “How fast was I going?”

I responded, “80 plus mph.”

He said, “There was no way this semi could go that fast.”

I said, “You truckers must be taught to say that, as every trucker I have stopped has said just that. He responded, have you ever heard of a governor?” I said, “Yes I have. He sits right there (pointing at the Capitol building to the north).

This comment set him off, saying, “I don’t mean that Governor.” I then asked for his vehicle information. He responded, “I’m not telling you.” so I climbed up into the driver’s seat of his semi with him yelling, “You can’t do that without a search warrant.”

I obtained the needed information for the tickets I was writing, while all the time he was ranting and raving. When the tickets were complete for the driver to sign, I handed him the completed tickets for speeding, following too closely, unsafe lane changes and asked him to sign his name to same and he refused.

I spun him around, putting handcuffs on him with some pulling and jerking. He shouted, “What are you doing?”

I stated, “Since you refused to sign for said traffic tickets, you are going to jail and the semi and load would be impounded.”

With this being said and done, while passing vehicles were honking and yelling “Yeh, Yah!” As these vehicles had been overtaken, tailgated and passed miles before.

This 18 wheel driver was getting what all of us felt was his just reward, which was probably long overdue and deserved many times over and over. **Officer Robert A. Lee**

Bumblebee Man

As Police, we see all kinds of injuries and deaths. We try to harden ourselves for it and be prepared for the next call, but sometimes it doesn't work. A lot of times we wind up making jokes about calls that were bad, just to keep from breaking down and crying.

Other times, we just can't help but smile at some of the stupid things people do to themselves.

I responded to a call with another Deputy to a residence in the country after a man had reported finding his neighbor dead. When I got there, I found the man lying face down on his bed, with his head on top of a bucket.

As we checked out the area and began investigating the death, we discovered that the man, who was naked, had been auto-eroticizing as he sniffed some sort of glue from the can. Apparently, he had huffed too much glue and passed out, with his head falling on the can. All this did was allow him to breathe even more fumes and he died of asphyxia.

The way the room was set up, you only had a small area to squeeze by next to a book case to get to the back of the bed. When I got to the rear of the bed, I could see a large stick protruding from the man's anal orifice. The man looked like a big bumblebee with a stinger protruding from his nether regions.

The State Police were called to investigate and one of the Investigators was a friend of mine. We did not tell him about the stick, but let him discover it for himself. The body was sent to the crime lab with the stick still protruding.

We will forever remember that call as the death of the "bumblebee man" What a way to be remembered.

Detective David

Cowboys & Indians

I received a complaint of speeding vehicles on a hilly residential street that intersected on both ends with a major thoroughfare. The speed limit was 30 mph.

I positioned myself so as not to be observed on the side of said street with a hand held radar unit obtaining the average safe speed as this was a hilly road with many side streets.

I observed a racing motorcycle cresting the hill at a very high rate of speed. The rider observed me and opened his throttle. I chased him but lost sight as his motorcycle was much lighter and more mobile than my motorcycle.

After turning into a residential area, going right and left on seventh street, I thought to Myself, *"What would I do if I were him?"* I slowed to a low speed and started checking driveways of homes. After a short while I observed his motorcycle laying on its side next to a pick-up truck.

I dismounted and walked up the driveway, looking for the rider. As I came closer to the pick-up, I observed the rider had laid his bike down and crawled underneath the pick-up.

He was lying flat on the ground.

I leaned over and looked at him. He said, "I guess I'm in trouble."

I said, "Yes, I believe you are!" I pulled him out from under the pick-up and cuffed him.

I asked him why he had laid his bike down. He said he thought I would not observe him on the motorcycle and that he did this because he did not want to go to jail.

I explained that because he ran, he was being arrested and his motorcycle impounded.

I called for a transport unit and a wrecker for his motorcycle.

While waiting for this, the arrested rider stated, “The Cowboys did this when they were being chased by the Indians.” And I said, “Son, you are not a Cowboy and I am not an Indian.”

Officer Robert A. Lee

Forgery

Detective Jim, who worked with Forgeries, was sharing a story about a man who broke into a home and stole some checks.

A few days later, the thief proceeded to go to the business of the homeowner that he had robbed and tried to cash a check - one of the very checks he had stolen.

It's a good thing that he didn't connect the name of the business and the name of the homeowner.

The employees knew of the robbery and called the police immediately.

You could say that justice was served as the robber was handcuffed and taken off to jail.

Detective Jim

Only In Texas

A lawyer ran a stop sign and got pulled over by a Texas Sheriff's Deputy. He thought that he was smarter than the deputy because he was a lawyer from New York and was certain that he had a better education than any cop from Podunk, Texas.

He decided to prove this to himself and have some fun at the Texas Deputy's expense.

The Deputy said, "License and registration, please."

"What for?" said the lawyer.

The deputy said, "You didn't come to a complete stop at the stop sign."

Then the lawyer said, "I slowed down, and no one was coming."

"You still did not come to a complete stop," said the deputy. "License and registration, please."

The lawyer said, "What's the difference?"

"The difference is you have to come to a complete stop, that's the law. License and registration, please." The Deputy repeated.

Next, the lawyer said "If you can show me the legal difference between slow down and stop, I'll give you my license and registration, and you give me the ticket…If not, you let me go and don't give me the ticket."

"That sounds fair. Please exit your vehicle, sir." the deputy said.

At this point, the deputy took out his nightstick and said, "using my nightstick as the example, would it be easier for you to understand the difference between stop and slow down if I were actually hitting you with the stick?”

God Bless Texas!

Search Warrant

We were going to execute a Search Warrant on a residence that contained a suspected meth lab. The occupant of the residence was known to have weapons and was already out on bond on other charges, so there was a higher than average threat level with this search.

Normally we try to get all the information that we can on the lay-out of the building to be searched, but in this instance, all we had to go on was a rough sketch by people that had been inside to get meth from the suspect, and they were not usually very skillful in describing things.

At the time we executed the Search Warrant, we knew that there was a living room first, followed by a kitchen, with a half wall in between the two rooms. A door leading to the laundry room was supposed to be on the right, with a hallway to the bedrooms on the left.

The meth lab was supposed to be in the laundry room, so this was a focal point of the search. We assumed that if the suspect was home, he could well be in the laundry room.

As we entered, we found the layout surprisingly accurate, including the door to the laundry room. This door was locked, so one of the Deputies rammed it with his shoulder to force it open, and ran into the room to secure it.

We heard the Deputy scream and the other Deputies assigned to support converged on that doorway…and looked in with amazement at a stairway leading to the basement, where the laundry room was located. The Deputy was at the bottom of the stairs, scuffed up, ripped pants and bruised ego, but otherwise O.K.

Thankfully, no one was home and no one was injured, other than falling down a set of stairs.

Angry Squirrel

I responded to a call of an alarm going off at this residence. Upon my arrival, I noticed that no vehicles were present and I saw something at the front window. As I got closer I could see that a 2.5 to 3 pound angry male squirrel was inside the blinds in the front window. The squirrel immediately struck a defiant posture with me and it appeared to be in top physical shape.

I reported my finding to dispatch and they informed me where a key was hidden and asked that I attempt to capture or force the fierce creature from the home.

When I unlocked the door, I found the home to be quite dark and I slowly entered, watching for a possible ambush from said squirrel. I found light switches and illuminated the home and discovered that the squirrel had taken a position of cover in the fireplace. As our gazes met, it was apparent that this squirrel would not go along peacefully. I worked my way around the couch and the squirrel reared back on his haunches and displayed his elongated teeth and claws. My attempts to reason with him were unsuccessful, so I decided it was time for hands-on. As I approached this surprisingly agile creature, it gave me a head fake and went towards the kitchen. Using all of my cat-like quickness, I lunged and caught it by the tail.

A brief skirmish took place as we rolled on the floor. However, due to my slight size advantage, I was able to wrestle it to the front door. I strongly reprimanded the squirrel for his trespassing and resisting apprehension and released it into the front yard. I secured the rest of the house and resumed patrol. No further action was required.

Sergeant Waring

Oh, That Finger

We were assisting the State Police and the Drug Task Force on a Search Warrant at a residence that reportedly had a large amount of marijuana being processed inside. I was third in line for the main entrance entry team, just behind the two Task Force officers who were familiar with the residence. Other Officers would follow with some staying outside to do perimeter security.

As the first Officer announced, “Police. Search Warrant,” he kicked the door and it just flew inside, with pieces of the door frame flying everywhere. He ran into the first room with the second Officer and me following.

Just as we entered, we could see someone sleeping on the couch. We had our weapons trained on him when pieces of the door frame fell back down. One of the pieces hit the second Officer right on his hand that held his pistol, knocking if from his grasp. The gun fell to the floor.

I had to continue in with the first Officer to secure the other areas of the small house, while additional Officers poured into the front room.

The Officer who dropped his gun was pointing his finger like a gun and yelling for the sleeping suspect to put up his hands. The suspect complied, saying, “Don’t Shoot!” over and over, and was taken into custody, having been captured with little more than a “loaded finger”.

Halloween

It was Halloween Night. The Fraternities from the University of Central Arkansas were having a contest to see which one could steal the most decorations from people's porches.

They were taking them to a parking lot at the City reservoir and made piles for each fraternity.

I hid my unmarked car and laid down in one of the piles of decorations and covered myself up.

When they arrived with the next load of plunder and started stacking it on top of me, they just about had heart attacks when the scare crow (me) came alive in the middle of the pile.

It was a kick to see the look on their faces and hear the gasps.

He Tried and Tried and Tried

After arresting both drivers in an accident for DWI, I recognized that one of the young men was the son of a local prominent attorney. Knowing that I needed to dot all my "I's" and cross my "T's", I did everything exactly correct. Arkansas Law states that after the suspect takes an alcohol test for law enforcement, they have the right to take a test at their own expense. Law enforcement is responsible for assisting them in obtaining that test.

After I concluded my paperwork, I transported the young lad to the local hospital for the test of his choice. Due to the number of times the hospital had been stiffed for the bill in similar instances, the hospital refused to give the test unless he paid for the test on the spot. I then took him to the ATM and he could not remember his PIN. I took him to his house and no one was home. I let him use my phone to call anyone he could think of for help but to no avail.

When he handed me my phone back, I asked him if there was anything else I could do to assist him, he said he had called everyone he could think of, including his "Dad's slut, FiFi". Of course, I was recording everything that was said.

His father represented him in court and asked me what assistance I had given in obtaining the second test. I detailed everything, including the quote about "his slut" and named her by name, not knowing that she was seated in the courtroom.

Needless to say, that ended the cross examination and she stomped out of the courtroom.

Nine – One – One

The complainant stated via a 911 call that a massive opossum was holding him hostage in his apartment. The complainant also said that he had a gun and wanted to know if he could shoot the opossum.

Dispatch advised against that action. I arrived and ascended the stairs to determine what sort of beast I was up against.

The eight pound plus opossum reared up on its hind legs and assumed a fighting position. I debated on the proper use of force and decided to put my safety aside and attempt pepper spray first.

As I was getting the pepper spray out, it charged me. I was instantly sorry I did not go for a bigger choice of weapon, but I used what I had. The opossum absorbed a large quantity of pepper spray but continued its charge.

Fighting against my own urge to retreat, I held my ground and wrestled the opossum to the bottom of the stairs.

The pepper spray must have started to take effect as the now dazed giant possum began to meander off toward the wooded area. I was thanked for my efforts and resumed patrol.

No further action was needed.

Sergeant Waring

Traffic Stop

I stopped a speeding van on an expressway. I approached the driver and asked the usual questions:

#1. Do you know why you are being stopped?

#2. Do you know how fast you were going?

#3. Do you have an emergency?

He said "no" to speed and speed limit, "no" to why he was being stopped and "yes" to an emergency. When asked what the emergency was – he replied that he had to pee badly and was jerking around in his seat.

I told him to go in the bushes between the expressway and the median. He got out of the driver's seat and immediately unzipped, pulled it out and urinated into the highway for everyone to see while passing us in broad daylight.

I placed him under arrest, called for a wrecker for his car and a transport unit. He was filed on, not only for traffic but also for disorderly conduct. How stupid is that!?!???

Officer Robert A. Lee

Meth Lab

We were going to serve a search warrant at a residence on a meth lab. I was in the lead vehicle and would be with the entry team to secure the residence before the search began.

We had a "rookie" officer with us and he begged to come and help, so I had him coming in the front door behind everyone else to keep him safe and give him a taste of the adventure he so craved.

As we approached the house, all of the vehicles sped up, with some cars going behind the residence so those officers could secure the back, while my vehicle took the front.

The rookie was following right behind me.

We had, I think, four of us in my vehicle. As I quickly stopped, we all began jumping out of the car to begin lining up for the entry. However, the rookie failed to stop and rammed the rear of my car just as we were exiting. The hit knocked every one of us down and we were all piled up in the front yard.

The rookie stood there in a panic, asking what to do next. All of us were dazed and I told the rookie to go ahead and get to the front door. He mistook this to mean "go ahead and enter the residence" which he promptly did, announcing his position and also giving some sort of "rebel yell" which scared the hell out of all of us, police and suspects alike.

After a few seconds, we were able to get up and get inside, and found that the officers in the rear of the house had seen the wreck and went ahead and made entry in the back.

We were able to find the lab and secure it, and arrested three suspects. Other than four officers with very sore necks and backs, and a bunch of everyone else still half deaf from a very loud scream, we all survived to do it again another day.

Mob Action

I started working for the Linn Township Police Department part time in the summer of 1956. It is located on the Wisconsin, Illinois State line. It is a perfect square, six miles by six miles with the north one quarter of the Township having a five thousand acre lake running through it from east to west, the rest of the land is rural and/or farmland. It is the lake which makes the Township unique in different ways. The lake is called Lake Geneva

and was called the Newport of the west because of the numerous millionaires who have estates on its shoreline. To name a few, the Wrigley family – chewing gum, Schwinn family – bicycles, Peterkin family – Morton Salt, Maytag family-washing Machines, Drake family- Drake Hotel, Griffith family – Abbott Laboratories, 70% of its shore line is within the jurisdiction of the Township. The lake is only 75 miles north of Chicago and ninety nine percent of the homes are owned by Chicago area people and are used primarily as summer retreats. The Township has thirty seven subdivisions; again, the homes are only used during the summer months.

Linn has a very low crime rate and so the majority of our police work is patrolling these subdivisions and the estates, consequently, we get to know the owners of the estates and many owners in the subdivisions on a personal basis. This is how I met a mobster who lived in one of the subdivisions.

There are a number of gangster or mobster families that enjoy living on the lake as well.

Lake Geneva is like Hot Springs, Arkansas. It is a neutral area. Warring families come to the lake to recreate with their families, they want no trouble nor do they make any trouble. As a new kid on the block, I got my first introduction to a mobster we'll call Bugsy.

It was evening and I was riding with the Chief. He said he was going to introduce me to a mobster and most likely there would be bodyguards with him. I was told to just act natural.

When we arrived at his house, we entered through the basement. Bugsy was in a regular barber's chair getting a shave and a haircut and there were two bodyguards with guns in shoulder holsters just standing around. The man doing the barbering also carried a gun.

Bugsy told one of the bodyguards to take the kid (me) up to his gun room. The room was probably 12' by 12' and there were guns of all kinds hanging on the walls. There were two bushel baskets full of pistols. To say the least, I was impressed and flabbergasted.

Down through the years, we had people complain about noise and fireworks during the 4th of July. Bugsy always had a big party on the 4th and had a permit to set off his fireworks. Every year there would be complaints from neighbors saying the fireworks dropped on their canvas boat covers burned holes in them. Bianco would ask us to talk with the complainants and find out what the damage was and how much it would cost to replace the boat covers. We'd find out and Bugsy would give us the cash to pay them off.

Bugsy was very patriotic, liked to celebrate the Fourth and money was no object for any repairs needed.

John L. Palmer

Topless

A short while after going topless was legalized and while working traffic before a football game in the University area, I was in the middle of a street directing traffic on the University Drag area. A Mustang convertible stopped right beside me. The vehicle contained two young women. Both driver and passenger were well endowed and topless.

The driver asked, "Officer, how do you like these?" while both were showing their breasts.

I was somewhat startled at this, but I stated, "I like….now keep your vehicle moving before we have a collision caused by gawkers and rubberneckers!"

Officer Robert A. Lee

Special Thank you to all my fellow Officers who contributed their funniest stories in Section Three of this book.

Contributing Officers

Bill McElwain

Bill Milburn

Detective David

Detective Jim

John L. Palmer

Officer Andrew

Officer Dwight

Officer Jack

Officer Mary (Sarg')

Officer Robert A. Lee

Sergeant Waring

Policeman's Prayer

Oh Lord, while I'm on my beat,
May I know that you're with me,
And protect me as I go to guard
Others' lives and property.

Help me ignore those who scorn
And show me no respect,
But be mindful of all citizens
I've sworn to protect

Be with my fellow officers
And guard their safety too.
May I always put duty first
In the work that I must do.

May I not disgrace the uniform
But bring pride to the badge I wear.
That I'd be a good policeman, Lord,
Would be my only prayer.
Amen.

Chief , Alexander Police Department

Cadiz, Kentucky.

We are Looking for a Few Great Stories!

Tony Cuttone is excited about getting started on Volume 2 of the **Insider Stories of the Chicago Police Force & Others** and he wants to invite his fellow Police Officers from around the country to send in your favorite, true, funny story for possible inclusion in the book.

Please limit your stories to 800 words or less,
Stories must be true,

As you can tell from some of the stories within, we aren't worried about being politically correct! These are stories for cops about cops.

So if you have a story that has a sense of humor, please send it to me at:

Tony Cuttone
P.O. BOX 816
Clinton, AR 72031

Even some stories that contain a total dumb person (and there are many), and their actions. If it is funny, we want to see it!

Selected stories will include your first name/rank, along with the state in which the story came from. For example;

Officer Bob, California.

If you have any questions, you can contact us at:
info@tonycuttone.com.

To order personally autographed books on-line,
Visit: http://tonycuttone.com

Quantity Ordered			**Total**
	"Insider Stories from the Chicago PF..."		
______	ISBN# 978-1-935122-37-1	$12.95	______
______	**Shipping & Handling**		______

($3.00 for 1st book ordered, $1.00 for each additional book)

Order Total ______

Mail your order with your check (U.S. funds only please) to:

Tony Cuttone,
PO Box 816
Clinton, AR 72031

Name: ______________________________
Shipping Address: ______________________________
City/State: ______________________________
Zip Code: ______________ E-mail address: ______________
Phone Number: ______________________________

If you have any questions, e-mail: info@tonycuttone.com

Made in the USA
San Bernardino, CA
19 July 2014